Third Eye Awakening

The Essential Guide to Achieving Higher Consciousness, New Perspectives, and Spiritual Awakening

Layla Moon

© Copyright 2022 - All rights reserved.

The content contained within this book may not be reproduced, duplicated or transmitted without direct written permission from the author or the publisher.

Under no circumstances will any blame or legal responsibility be held against the publisher, or author, for any damages, reparation, or monetary loss due to the information contained within this book, either directly or indirectly.

Legal Notice:

This book is copyright protected. It is only for personal use. You cannot amend, distribute, sell, use, quote or paraphrase any part, or the content within this book, without the consent of the author or publisher.

Disclaimer Notice:

Please note the information contained within this document is for educational and entertainment purposes only. All effort has been executed to present accurate, up-to-date, reliable, and complete information. No warranties of any kind are declared or implied. Readers acknowledge that the author is not engaged in the rendering of legal, financial, medical, or professional advice. The content within this book has been derived from various sources. Please consult a licensed professional before attempting any techniques outlined in this book.

By reading this document, the reader agrees that under no circumstances is the author responsible for any losses, direct or indirect, that are incurred as a result of the use of the information contained within this document, including, but not limited to, errors, omissions, or inaccuracies.

Table of Contents

INTRODUCTION 1

   CHAKRAS: A BRIEF HISTORY 2
      The Westernization of Chakras 2

MY JOURNEY 5

   HOW THIS GUIDE CAN HELP YOU 6
   THE REAL QUESTION 7

CHAPTER 1: AWAKENING THE THIRD EYE 9

   THE SEVEN CHAKRAS 10
      Nervous Systems 11
      Spirling Pools of Energy 11
      The Root Chakra 12
      The Sacral Chakra 12
      The Solar Plexus Chakra 13
      The Heart Chakra 13
      The Throat Chakra 14
      The Third Eye Chakra 14
      The Crown Chakra 15

PINEAL GLAND AND ITS SIGNIFICANCE 17

      The Center of the Soul 17
      Melatonin 18
      Calcification of the Pineal Gland 19
   CLOSED EYE SYMPTOMS 20
      Blockage 20
      Symptoms 21
   POTENTIAL DANGERS 22
      Precautions: Spiritual Guides 23
      Precautions: Open Your Other Chakras First 24
      Nightmares 24

- *Delusions* *25*
- KEY TAKEAWAYS 25

CHAPTER 2: 10 STEPS TO AWAKENING 29

- CEMENT YOUR INTENT 30
  - *Affirmations*.. *31*
- MEDITATE 32
  - *Breathing* *33*
  - *Visualization of Colors* *33*
- PRACTICE SOUND THERAPY 34
  - *Chanting* *35*
- DO SOME YOGA 35
  - *Child's Pose* *36*
  - *Head to Knee Pose*... *36*
  - *Warrior Pose*.. *37*
  - *Locust Pose* *37*
- EMBRACE THE NATURAL WORLD... 38
  - *The Illusion of Separation* *39*
  - *Exercise*... *40*
  - *Sun and Moon Gazing* *41*
- WRITE DOWN YOUR DREAMS 42
- GET OUT OF YOUR COMFORT ZONE 43
  - *Travel*.. *43*
  - *New Hobbies and Activities* *44*
- EAT HEALTHY FOODS 46
  - *Fruits and Vegetables*... *46*
  - *Foods to Avoid* *47*
- UTILIZE CRYSTALS... 48
- ENHANCE WITH ESSENTIAL OILS 49
- KEY TAKEAWAYS 50

CHAPTER 3: WHAT TO EXPECT 53

- MASLOW'S HIERARCHY OF NEEDS 53
- OPENED THIRD EYE 55
- BENEFITS OF AWAKENING YOUR THIRD EYE 56
  - *Achieved Higher Consciousness*.................................... *56*
  - *Intuition Improvement*.. *57*
  - *Positive Outlook*... *58*

- *Lucid Dreaming* 59
- *Psychic Abilities* 59
- POSSIBLE NEGATIVE EXPERIENCES 60
  - *Headaches* 61
  - *Nightmares and Sleeping Difficulties* 61
  - *Sensory Overload* 62
  - *Fear and Anxieties* 62
  - *Astral Projection* 63
- SPIRITUAL AWAKENING 64
  - *Closing Your Third Eye* 65
- KEY TAKEAWAYS 66

CONCLUSION 69

- BEFORE AWAKENING 69
- 10 STEPS TO AWAKENING 70
- AFTER AWAKENING 72
- REFLECT ON YOUR JOURNEY 73

REFERENCES 75

Introduction

Leonardo da Vinci once said, "There are three classes of people: those who can see, those who can see when shown, and those who cannot see." Although the context was completely different from today, his words still ring with truth. Once my third eye was unblocked, it was easy to see who had reached their spiritual enlightenment and who had not.

Spiritual awakening, especially opening your chakras and opening your third eye, is an intense experience that many people do not dare to undergo. It changes who you are at a fundamental level, creating self-awareness and understanding of what you can achieve. It is one of the most terrifying experiences, but you also receive the most rewards.

If you've picked up this book, you are, at the bare minimum, vaguely aware of chakras and the third eye. Chakras are the centers of energy within the body. There are seven main chakra centers in the body and can be attributed to many physical ailments, which will be covered more in-depth in the next chapter of this book. For now, I will be discussing the historical context of chakra healing.

Chakras: A Brief History

The first writings of chakras were initially introduced in text ranging from 1500-500 BCE in a yogas text known as the Vedas. Many Indian scholars and historians believe that the knowledge of chakras was passed down through oral traditions and practices. These practices rippled down from generation to generation, cultivating an entirely new belief system. The chakra philosophy emphasizes that the universe was created and maintained by two equal but opposite forces. This is similar to yin and yang in ancient Chinese culture. These forces are called Shakti and Shiva. Shiva is the embodiment of absolute consciousness while Shiva is the "personification of the universe" (Schneider 23). 'Chakra,' a Sanskrit word meaning 'wheel,' is first mentioned in the ancient Vedas text.

While the Vedas is only one of the texts, throughout the millennia there have been other texts from yoga dating as far back as 600 BCE. The Yoga Upanishads and the Yoga Sutras of Patanjali of 200 BCE discuss the spiritualism of chakras. These texts are the forefathers of the spiritual aspect of chakras we know today.

The Westernization of Chakras

The chakras we know of today are the product of several texts ranging from the 10th century to the early 1900s. They are the trifecta of our foundation for the knowledge of the seven main chakras. One of the texts known as *Gorakshashatakam* gives comprehensive instructions for meditating on chakras. In 1577, the text called *Sat-Cakra-Nirupan* by Swami Purnananda gives the reader an understanding of each chakra center. The last of the three foundational texts was written in 1919 by Sir John Woodroffe known as *The Serpent Power*. This book builds on the foundations of the previous texts and modernizes them into modern practices. It introduced chakra theory to the West.

Although this practice was slow to gain traction at first, within the past thirty years, chakra and spiritualism have become a staple to achieving higher consciousness and peace within. With the decreasing faith in religion, chakra theory has evolved into an almost-mainstream practice.

My Journey

One of the reasons you picked up this book is because you want to know how to awaken your third eye. You want to feel like a more complete human and ascend into another plane of existence. This is an important part of the process of awakening your spirituality. Religion, whether it is Christianity, Islam, or Buddhism, does not work for you. You have not felt the connection to a supreme being in the universe, but you still want to have spirituality within your life. Opening your sixth chakra, also known as the third eye, can help with this.

I have felt the same way. About a decade ago, I was in the depths of despair: a divorce, losing key members of my family, and financial hardships crippled me. I was at one point a devout Catholic, but I did not feel a spiritual connection to God the way my family described. For about five years, I felt like a failure to my family and my faith, further isolating me from my family and friends.

During this isolation, I focused on myself and my journey. It was not the glorious self-care as is portrayed in social media these days. It felt like an insurmountable mountain, and I was at the foot of it. It was not taking bubble baths and reading my favorite book to escape my current fate. It took a lot of work and the obliteration of my comfort zone. When traveling, I learned to meditate thanks to some of my hostel roommates. When I returned home, I felt more whole and fulfilled.

Meditating, in conjunction with travel, helped me to reflect on what was important to me. I was no longer religious, which held an extensive backlash from friends and family. Eventually, some of us made peace with mutual respect for each individual's journey. In other cases, the relationship ended, and we went our separate ways.

Despite these negative experiences with friends and a few members of my family, I would not change anything about my spirituality. I am whole and complete. I would not be the woman I am today without awakening my true self.

How This Guide Can Help You

I am hopeful you have not gone through the same situations as I have. Oftentimes, how others perceive us is a reflection of how we see ourselves. When you open your third eye, along with the rest of your chakras, your life will change for the better. No longer will you need validation from others. You can start the process of becoming your best self.

This comprehensive guide can help you gain an understanding of your third eye, how to unblock this chakra, and what to expect: both the positives and the negatives. There are ten steps I recommend in order to fully awaken your third eye. Eight of these steps you can implement during meditation and yoga, such as embracing the natural world and sound therapy. Dream journaling can be done for ten minutes upon waking. Getting out of your comfort zone will take some time and planning, such as traveling and trying out new activities and hobbies. I will also recommend four yoga poses and meditation practices.

Most of the practices and recommendations of this book do not require additional purchases, but instead offer practical advice to implement into your daily life. Some items, such as crystals and essential oils, will help to enhance the experience, but are not required to awaken your third eye.

The Real Question

The real question here is: Are you ready to open your third eye?

Think for a second about what this can mean to you. You can have wonderful experiences by awakening your third eye. There are many benefits such as increased intuition and a positive outlook on life. Your life will be able to control your dreams, and therefore, you will have more self-control. You may even be gifted with psychic powers. Your life will now reflect the spiritual awakening you have experienced.

Be warned, however, that there can be negative consequences to opening your third eye before it is ready to. Do not force your third eye to open, lest you will have potential negative side effects such as nightmares and unwanted astral projections. There are real dangers to opening your third eye if you are not ready.

I will reiterate this often: this is a process and not a one-and-done event. It is a continual habit that will lead you to the mental and physical space you want to be in. Awakening your third eye is essentially a lifestyle change. You must be open and want the change for it to truly happen. If you are committed to this process, keep reading to learn more about how to implement these practices.

I will ask again.

Are you ready?

Chapter 1:

Awakening the Third Eye

"Be warned: opening the chakras is an intense experience," says Guru Pathik in the show called *Avatar: The Last Airbender*. The show originally aired on Nickelodeon in 2005 and has since then awakened a curiosity in chakras in its audience. I watched the show when it first aired and loved it. Although I was older than its targeted audience, the show was recommended to me by a friend whose children were obsessed with it.

It follows the journey of Aang, a young Airbender who awakens from his one-hundred-year slumber to a world ravaged by war with the Fire Nation. He must master the bending of the four elements: air, water, earth, and fire, as well as his most powerful state known as the Avatar State. The Avatar State is a compilation of his past lives, who were also previous Avatars, and their knowledge and wisdom. He must defeat the tyrant Firelord Ozai and bring balance to the world.

The second season called *Book Two: Earth* aired in 2006, and that is where the seven chakras are introduced. To master the Avatar State, he must clear the blockages in his seven chakras to awaken the ability to go in and out of the Avatar State at will. In the episode called "The Guru," he meets with Guru Pathik, who mentors him on how to clear his chakras. He eventually succeeds to master the Avatar State and defeats Ozai in the last season.

Avatar: The Last Airbender is a great show on many levels, but for our purposes here, it is a wonderful introduction to the seven chakras. It was initially what enticed me to explore spiritual awakening in my own life after the many years of strife I experienced. The difference between the show and reality is that Aang can open all his chakras in less than ten minutes. Note that this is not how it works; it can often take weeks, months, and even years to achieve the wholeness and power Aang was able to unlock. However, it can guide us to what each chakra is.

The Seven Chakras

According to chakra expert Anodea Judith, "the chakra system is a profound philosophical system that represents the levels of consciousness. So it's the map to the architecture of your soul" (2022). Each of the seven chakras has its meaning, color, and location. Although the show does speak of a specific color in correlation to its chakra, the images in which Aang must overcome the blockages are ripe with each color's association.

Nervous Systems

Each chakra is located in an integral part of the central nervous system. Science is now validating some of the aspects associated with chakras. The two nervous systems within the body deal with vital organs and nerves located in each of the seven chakras. The central nervous system (CNS) primarily focuses on the brain and spine. The peripheral nervous system (PNS) focuses on the organs and nerves, which are then connected to the brain and spine. The PNS is also divided into two separate smaller systems, the somatic and autonomic systems. Somatic includes voluntary movements such as moving your limbs. The autonomic includes automated actions such as breathing, heartbeats, and digestion.

The autonomic system is where each chakra is located. Each chakra is located in different parts of the spine and the organs that are around the area. The chakras are associated with different aspects of each part of the nervous system as a whole. Sensations such as defecation, sexual arousal, and urination are a part of the chakras and balancing them. To balance our third eye, it is imperative to balance out the rest of our bodies like a well-oiled machine. Without grease and maintenance, the body is prone to falling apart.

Spirling Pools of Energy

Guru Pathik teaches Aang to picture chakras and the energy within us like spirling pools in a creek. If there is a blockage in even one of the pools, the water cannot flow. This causes the water to become murky and stagnant. However, if you remove the blockage, the water can flow down the creek. The energy within our bodies and spirits is similar to the swirling pools, which help the creek run freely. As mentioned previously, the word chakra means 'wheel.' This refers to how the energy swirls in one of the seven main locations within the body.

Before we can open and awaken the third eye, it is imperative to first open the first five chakras.

The Root Chakra

This is the first chakra, also known as the grounding chakra, that needs to be opened. It is located at the base of the spine and deals with basic survival instincts. It is blocked by anxieties and fear for your survival. This chakra is balanced when you feel comfortable and safe. This chakra is associated with the adrenal gland, which releases hormones throughout the body, as well as balances your metabolism. These hormones can be adrenaline, cortisol, and the sex hormones known as gonads. The color associated with the root chakra is red while the element is earth. To proceed with clearing the other chakras, you will need to become grounded, hence the name and its affiliation to earth.

The Sacral Chakra

The second chakra is located in the pelvic region where the sexual organs are, along with the lower back and abdomen. This chakra deals with pleasure and the biological need for reproduction. Sensuality, sexuality, creative expression, and emotions are also related to this chakra. It is blocked by emotional guilt and sexual repression. Sexual repression is the inability to express your sexuality. It is also the center where your creativity flows. Anything related to what gives you pleasure is this chakra. It is balanced when you feel creative and sexual pleasure fulfillment. The color associated with the sacral chakra is orange, and its element is water.

The Solar Plexus Chakra

The third chakra is located around your belly button and deals with your ego and self-confidence. Even though the root chakra produces the hormones needed for digestion, your stomach and solar plexus area are where your digestion is. It is blocked by shame, and you may deal with digestive and intestinal issues. This is balanced with boundary-setting and bravery. When the chakra is balanced, your self-confidence and personal power will improve, as well as your digestion. The color associated with this chakra is yellow, and its element is fire.

The Heart Chakra

The heart chakra is located around your heart and deals with love in all its forms: friends, family, and romantic/sexual partners. The heart chakra is associated with the thymus gland, which creates and stores white blood cells. Your immune system is the center of this chakra. When you are feeling loved, you tend to feel healthier and can fight off infections. It is blocked by grief or feeling unloved and unappreciated. It is balanced when you give and receive love. Compassion and empathy are the cores of being able to give and receive love; therefore, healthy relationships are key here. The color associated with the fourth chakra is green, and its element is air.

The Throat Chakra

The throat chakra is located in the middle of the throat and deals with vocal self-expression or truth. While this mainly belongs to the throat, the chakra is also associated with the thyroid and sinuses. The thyroid is the gland that also utilizes the hormones associated with protein production and distribution within the body. It is blocked by the inability to properly communicate and the lies we tell ourselves. The throat chakra deals with communication and self-expression. It is balanced when you can communicate with others and speak your truth. The color associated with the throat chakra is a light blue, and its element is sound.

The Third Eye Chakra

The third eye chakra is located in between the eyes and deals with insight. Its main gland is the pineal gland and hypothalamus, which is located in the brain. Vision—both physical and metaphysical—is the key here. It is blocked by internal turbulence such as doubt and illusion. It is balanced when you connect to your inner thoughts. The color of the third eye chakra is indigo, and its element is light. We will go over more physical aspects of the pineal gland in the next section.

The Crown Chakra

The last chakra is located at the top of your head and deals with consciousness in its purest form. This chakra is symbolic of clear thought, a connection to the universe, and self-awareness. It is blocked by earthly attachments, and the emphasis is to let go of all attachments. There can be no true love or connection without realizing everything passes. It is balanced when you connect to the universe. The color of the crown chakra is either violet or white, while its element is thought.

In psychology, there is a theory of levels of fulfillment in a person's life. Instead of the seven chakras, there are five tiers in Maslow's Hierarchy of Needs. There will be an entire section dedicated to its explanation in Chapter 3.

Pineal Gland and its Significance

Now that we know the foundations of the chakras, we can now have an in-depth discussion of the third eye chakra. As mentioned, the third eye is located in between the eyes. However, this chakra also extends into the part of the brain called the pineal gland. It is a pinecone-shaped gland that sits in between your eyes and is responsible for the secretion of melatonin within the body.

The Center of the Soul

Even up until as recently as the 1950s, little was known about the pineal gland in the brain. In various cultures throughout history, the pineal gland was thought to be the resting place of the soul. Throughout history, from the ancient Egyptians to the ancient Greeks, the pineal gland was known as the "third eye." The third eye was representative of the soul and could see the truths of the universe. If the third eye was not opened, the person could see the truths and ascend to higher consciousness.

The ancient Egyptians called the third eye "the Eye of Horace," which was symbolic of healing and recovery.

Similarly, opening the third eye can lead to both of these symbolic attributes. In Hinduism, it is believed that the pineal gland was once a literal third eye that later deteriorated as part of their spiritual awakening.

In the early to mid-1600s, Descartes famously believed that the pineal gland was where the body, mind, and soul all joined. He also hypothesized that the gland was where thoughts and dreams are created. In his publication *La Dioptrique* in 1637, he illustrates how the pineal gland was connected to the nervous system.

Melatonin

The pineal gland is also responsible for its role in producing melatonin, a chemical within the brain that helps you fall asleep. When the pineal gland is producing melatonin normally, the brain typically wakes up with the sun rising and starts to wind down when the sun is setting. When the production is interrupted, irregular sleeping patterns start to occur such as too much sleep or insomnia.

Since the pineal gland is located in the middle of the forehead, it is the epicenter of all the energy within the body, and therefore can control that energy. The third eye's connection to the pineal gland transforms that energy into cosmic energy.

Calcification of the Pineal Gland

The pineal gland is susceptible to calcification, which is an excessive buildup of calcium phosphate crystals in various parts of the body. This could be a potential reason for the blockage of the third eye. When there is a buildup of these calcium phosphate crystals, it is often the product of foods that possess excessive amounts of calcium. Foods with additives, sugars, artificial sweeteners, and fluoride are the main culprits. This is toxic to our bodies and should be avoided when you can.

Calcification can also occur because of cell phone usage. There is also a theory that the radiation emitted from cell phone usage also increases third eye blockage. The blue light that emits from your phone halts the production of melatonin in the brain. Since the pineal gland is responsible for melatonin production, it is not much of a stretch to think excessive cell phone usage can hinder your progress in opening your third eye. Have you ever noticed that when you use your phone while trying to fall asleep, you have a hard time doing so? This is because your brain still thinks it is daytime from the cold blue light. Sleep experts recommend putting away your phone for at least an hour before bedtime so your brain can start to wind down.

To decalcify your pineal gland, changing your diet is recommended. There is more about what foods to remove from your diet, as well as what foods to eat, in the next chapter. The gist of it is to add more fresh fruits and vegetables to your diet.

Closed Eye Symptoms

Now that we know a little more in-depth knowledge of what the third eye is, how do we know whether it is blocked or not? Since you are still here with me, I can assume you have some inkling as to whether your third eye chakra is blocked or not. Some of the symptoms can be linked to mood disorders such as depression and bipolar disorder. Your third eye blockage can manifest in many different ways in both physical and mental suffering.

Blockage

Blockage stems from an imbalance within yourself and your ego. Once the third eye is opened, you will be able to see the things your ego will not allow you to see. The blockage can come from any form of hardship or feelings of inadequacy. For me personally, it was a compilation of the loss of a beloved family member, my divorce, and the years of financial hardship that was the cause of it. I was going through transitional life phases all at once, causing my third eye chakra to become unbalanced.

It does not have to be just a transformative phase, however. Your employment, and even the hobbies you enjoy, can also be a source of your imbalance. Say you're an artist, but then someone close to you discredits your work. This can not only be hurtful, but it can also throw your third eye out of balance.

Recognizing your third eye imbalance is one of the most important steps in order to fully awaken your third eye. Since we now know why the blockages can happen, let us talk about how to recognize the symptoms.

Symptoms

The symptoms of third eye blockage can manifest both physically and mentally. This is your body and your chakra telling you, "Something is wrong, and I need you to fix it." Listen to your intuition here and take the time you need to implement strategies to become more whole. Most of these symptoms are also attributed to depression and anxiety. Although opening your third eye can help you deal with the symptoms of depression, please keep in mind that it is not a substitute for mental healthcare professionals.

Some of the mental symptoms are as follows:

- Insignificance: perhaps it is within your career or personal life, but something feels off.

- Indecisiveness: this can impact which paths to follow will be best for you.

- Unfulfillment: your life feels dull and boring, and you feel as though something is missing.

- Narrow-mindedness: you are only focused on what is directly in front of you instead of the bigger picture.

The physical symptoms can manifest as follows:

- Headaches, especially migraines, are more frequent.

- Back and leg pain.

- Eye pain or discomfort.

- Abnormal sleeping patterns: oversleeping or insomnia

Notice these physical symptoms are related directly to either the brain or nervous system. Since the pineal gland is at the forefront of the brain, it is an integral part of the third eye. Therefore, these symptoms manifest in direct contact with the brain.

Potential Dangers

Even though the opening of your third eye can be a positive experience, it is imperative to know the potential dangers and side effects that can occur. Opening any of the chakras can be an intense experience, and the third eye is no exception to the rule. This typically happens when you are not fully ready to open the chakra. This is why it is imperative to not open this chakra before you are ready.

Precautions: Spiritual Guides

Before awakening the third eye, you may want to have a spiritual guide with you as you go through this process. Spiritual guides help you to open and maintain the chakra without navigating this process by yourself. You may want to do some research on a spiritual guide and interview them beforehand. Find someone who you trust and has had the type of experience before, whether they have gone through the experience themselves or have guided others. Guides can help you determine what areas and practices to focus on the most while enhancing your experience.

I recommend a guide. There is nothing wrong with independence, but when you are not an expert, it is best to have a mentor. My spiritual guide helped me understand what I needed in my personal growth and development, which helped me to unlock my potential with my third eye.

Your best offense to the powerful experience of opening your third eye is not to do this alone. This is your ego speaking to you. There is no need to go alone; it is better to have a second opinion and thoughts on the matter than to traipse through it by yourself. Just as is true when you experience hardships, you will not get any better until you have a connection with trusted family members, friends, and/or romantic partners. The same is true for your spiritual awakening.

Precautions: Open Your Other Chakras First

Another precaution to take is to open all the chakras before opening this one. If you do, you will be prone to negative experiences such as nightmares and even delusions. Do not force this chakra open. Typically, the ideal time of your life for opening your third eye is the ages of 35-45. At this point in your life, you will have enough experience and are more in tune with who you are. This does not mean you cannot achieve a higher consciousness at a younger age, but it may be more difficult for you to do so. Do not be discouraged. If you feel you are ready for this intense and rewarding experience, then do so. However, make sure you open the others first before attempting this.

Nightmares

There can be many physical ailments that come from awakening your third eye before you are ready. Headaches and migraines are among the most common. The worst—and more terrifying—are the nightmares and delusions that can follow. When you are in a low vibrational state or have not opened the other chakras beforehand, you are more susceptible to seeing beings you are not accustomed to.

Nightmares manifest as you see the horrors that can take shape in the waking world. Your nightmares will become much more vivid and realistic. Some people, when awakening their third eye without a guide or before opening their previous chakras, can report the inability to sleep at night. Some refuse to sleep at all. This can cause a plethora of health and psychological problems, including the result of seeing delusions.

Delusions

Those who experience delusions often state they have seen beings not of this world. The lines between reality and perceived reality. Fourth-dimensional beings walk among us, but if you open the sixth chakra too early or too quickly, you will still be able to sense them. Most of the beings are not friendly, and that will cause an increase in fear and paranoia within you. The line between fiction and reality will become blurred.

There will be a more in-depth section on what to do if you have negative experiences opening your third eye in Chapter 3.

Key Takeaways

Now that you've learned in great detail what the third eye is and some of the precautions, let us take a minute to summarize.

- There are seven main chakras within the human body: the root chakra, the sacral chakra, the solar plexus chakra, the heart chakra, the throat chakra, the third eye chakra, and the crown chakra.

- Each chakra is a step towards self-actualization.

- The process must begin with opening the first chakra, or root chakra.

- The pineal gland in the brain is the location of the third eye chakra. It produces melatonin and is believed to be the center of the soul. You should also limit the use of your cell phone, especially before bed.

- Closed eye symptoms are those associated with the brain and nervous system; headaches and back pain are the most common physical symptoms, while mental symptoms can be associated with depression.

- Blockage can occur by hardship and not being your true, authentic self.

- It is crucial to not awaken your third eye until you are ready. Use the help of a spiritual guide on your journey.

- Potential dangers and threats to awakening your third eye before you are ready are nightmares and delusions.

If you have found your spiritual guide and have opened your other chakras, you are now ready to start implementing this book as a guide for you to experience your third eye awakening.

Chapter 2:

10 Steps to Awakening

According to Susan Brunton, a master of all things metaphysical, opening your third eye is more of a drawn-out process and commitment than a singular occurrence. She says, "You don't just open it and move on with your life. You begin a journey of preparation and move steadily along the path towards opening it" (2022). There are many steps to take for your third eye awakening, but I have narrowed down the top ten that have worked best for me personally.

When I was on this journey myself, it helped to have not only a spiritual guide, but to have a community with me. One of my awakened friends recommended purchases of stones, crystals, and essential oils to help enhance the experience. I have added these three last to this list because I believe the core activities such as cementing your intent and getting out of your comfort zone will help you more than crystals and stones.

Remember that this is *your* journey. I am only here to give advice and my recommendations for the things that have worked for me.

Cement Your Intent

When you cement your intent, you are telling yourself and the universe what it is you are setting out to achieve. The intent is the first step to an awakened third eye because, without it, you will not achieve your goals. The root of any goal is your *why*. Why are you doing this? Answer. If you need to, write down your whys so you can refer to them later. Writing down your intention will help you traverse through the murky beginning. For example, ask yourself *why* it is that you want to awaken your third eye. Your answer could be *because I want to feel whole again after my divorce*. Your self-love and opening of your heart chakra will help you in this specific example, but your reasons will be your own. If your *why* is strong enough, your commitment will follow through with you.

The intent of meditation and yoga is also a very powerful technique to use. Before starting with the physical techniques, sit down in a quiet place where you usually meditate. Open your mind to the rest of the world. Your intent for the day will help to clarify what your goal is. For example, you can say things such as, "Today I will be calmer about my situation," or "My intention for the day is to be more creative." When you speak about what you will do for the day, it will help you face the challenges the day presents. Affirmations are also another technique to implement.

Affirmations

To affirm your intentions, you are expressing your strong belief in awakening your third eye. After you cement your intentions, stay seated in your position. Close your eyes and slow your breathing. This is also true for meditation, which we will go over in the next section. Take three deep breaths in through your nose and let them out slowly through your mouth. This will help calm you so you can see and think more clearly. Then speak your affirmations. Relax before speaking each affirmation.

There is no minimum or maximum limit to the number of affirmations you can have, but I recommend at least five. This is flexible depending on your schedule and what you can fit in.

Some examples can be:

- "I trust myself and my intuition."
- "I can see the beauty around me."
- "My third eye is open."
- "My motivation will help me power through this day."
- "I am connected to my expanded consciousness."
- "I am ready to expand on my intuition."
- "I trust myself and can flourish."

- "I am strong, I am important, I am brave."

You can also come up with your affirmations. What can you think of right now? Write them down and implement them. The more you affirm yourself, the more in-tune you are to yourself and the universe around you. This is also important because you are validating yourself when you speak these affirmations. Self-validation is important to open your third eye. When you affirm and validate yourself, self-worth increases, and your ability to perceive your third eye increases.

The next step is to meditate on these affirmations.

Meditate

When you meditate, you are emptying all your thoughts and focusing on one specific thing. This can be a reflection of your affirmations or intention, but it can also be where you visualize colors and associations with your third eye. Since you are already settled in a comfortable position, you can focus on your breathing and the subject you would like to meditate on.

Listening to soothing music can help you meditate. I recommend ambient noises such as ocean waves or rain. Music played on the piano, or the gentle strumming of a guitar helps me to hone in on the thoughts I want to focus on.

Be wary of concentrating too hard: you may end up with intense headaches. Let your mind be still. Set a timer for the amount of time you want to meditate; at least ten to twenty minutes should suffice. Cross your legs and close your eyes. And then, breathe.

Breathing

Breathing is the foundation of all mediation practices. It allows you to relax as you empty your mind of all things you do not want to focus on. As mentioned in the previous section, focusing on your breathing will help to calm you as you prepare for your meditation. Take three deep breaths: inhale through your nose, hold for a few seconds, then exhale through your mouth. As you breathe, allow the thoughts except for the things you want to focus on to melt away. For awakening your third eye, breathing can help to also visualize colors.

Focusing on the present moment is a byproduct of your breathing. You are grounding yourself in reality and cannot be moved by fictional delusions.

Visualization of Colors

The color mainly associated with the third eye chakra is indigo, but violet is another possible option. As the other thoughts evaporate like mist in the sun, focus on the color indigo. The moon can be a powerful symbol of indigo as it embodies themes of purity. When your third eye is open, you will be able to detect the truth, and therefore, the pureness of those around you.

As you visualize the color indigo, let the color wash over you until it is the only thing you can see in your mind's eye. You can do this by visualizing foods such as blueberries and eggplant, or even just the color itself. Allow the color to remove any negative feelings you may have, and you will release the blockages. What I typically visualize is a violet ball of energy from in between my eyes circulating down my body until it is released from the bottom of my feet. Allowing this visualization helps me with my blockages.

Do not be discouraged if you fail the first few times in visualizing the energy within you. This is a skill that can take a while to learn. Your spiritual guide can help you with more visualization techniques and more personalized techniques for you.

Practice Sound Therapy

While you are meditating, silence is a viable option. In many cases, adding sounds to your meditation can help with relaxation and the stimulation of your pineal gland. Humming or chanting stimulates your pineal gland through vibrations. You can also listen to music to transport you to a deep relaxation mode while meditating. This is called your theta state. You can either find playlists of theta-inducing music online or make some yourself if you have the capability to. What I have found most useful for me is chanting.

Chanting

When my spiritual guide first mentioned chanting to me, my mind went straight to cults and their chanting. However, this is far from what I mean by chanting. Chanting in this context means repeating a mantra over again while in meditation. This can be one of your affirmations, but it can also be simply enunciating "om" out loud. This sound should be long and drawn-out. Inhale, hold your breath, then exhale by saying "ooommmmm." The vibrations from the "mm" sound help with the stimulation of the pineal gland. You can also say "ahm" by following the same enunciation principle as "om." With either of these, you will be stimulating the pinecone-shaped gland located in the middle of your forehead. Repeat the process of breathing, visualizations, and sounds until your timer stops. Now that your timer has gone off, it is time to pull out your yoga mat and start with some poses.

Do Some Yoga

Yoga is a tried and true way to stretch your body and clear your mind. Yoga is for those who wish to practice mindfulness and explore their body's limits. Third eye poses are no exception to this and will help to open your third eye. In many of the poses, you are stretching your back, and therefore strengthening your spine and back muscles. As we already know, the back is one of the key components to your third eye awakening. With the yoga poses mentioned next, you may start to feel your third eye opening after you are finished with them after utilizing them for a while.

Many poses can be found online, but there are four I would recommend. These four yoga poses are the basics, and you can either look online or go to a yoga class to find out more poses unique to your capabilities and comfort.

Child's Pose

The first pose that I like to do is called the child's pose. It can help with your connection to your breathing. This is also a form of a fetal position and nourishes relaxation and warmth while stretching your back.

To do this pose, sit on your knees and lean forward until your head rests on the mat. You should feel your back stretching, and your breathing evens out. It also protects your vital organs, shielding you from any perceived threat or danger.

Head to Knee Pose

The second pose is called the head to knee pose, which is pretty self-explanatory. It can help you reflect on the moment and your feelings in the present moment. While in this pose, do not force the stretch; instead, focus on your intuition and breathing regulation.

To do this pose, simply sit on your mat and extend one of your legs while keeping the other tucked in towards your body. Rest your head on your knee and count to ten. This stretch opens your hips while increasing the strength in your hamstrings and back. It can also help ease the pain of menstrual and menopausal issues.

Warrior Pose

The warrior pose is one of the most common in yoga known for its simplicity. It works out and stretches your shoulders, hips, and legs. It can also help with lung problems. While you are in this pose, focus on the energy within you as it relaxes you.

To do the warrior pose, you first stand on your mat and slide one of your legs backward. It does not matter which one. Bend your opposite knee forward 90 degrees while keeping your back straight. Hold the stance as you extend your arms from your sides. Raise your arms over your head slowly until they meet above your head. Hold the pose for about five to ten seconds and release. When you are finished, repeat with the opposite leg.

Locust Pose

The last pose I recommend is the locust pose for beginners. It is an easy stretch that can strengthen your shoulders, your back muscles, and your core. Keep focusing on your breathing and do not strain yourself in this pose, which can be easy to do.

To do the locust pose, lay flat on your stomach with your forehead and the tops of your feet resting on the mat. Inhale and slowly raise your chest and head along with your legs, starting with your thighs, in the air. Then hold the pose as you breathe slowly. After you finish holding the pose, slowly lower your legs and chest until you are lying flat on the mat again.

If you cannot concentrate on both at once, focus instead on raising just your chest and head, then hold the pose.

For all the poses, it is important to note that when you are first starting, do not strain yourself or do more than what your body can handle at the moment. You may injure yourself. Remember the goal here is to stretch out your muscles and relax. If there are certain parts of each pose you cannot do because of your body's limitations, that is okay. Over time, your body will strengthen, and you will become more advanced in your yoga poses. The key is to start and make the commitment.

If you want to knock out two birds with one stone, so to speak, consider doing these yoga exercises outside. Coincidentally, the next step is to spend more time outside.

Embrace the Natural World

To fully awaken your sixth chakra, you should spend more time outside. Communing with nature helps to align your chakra and will help you understand the balance between yourself and the earth. Now, this does not mean you should go and run naked through the woods, but even simply removing your shoes and socks to feel the earth beneath you should be enough. Sit with the earth and feel its vibrations and meditate on the world around you. Breathe in the fresh air and surrender yourself to the pleasure. The heat of the sun warms you; the rain washes away your worries. If it is snowing, go outside and play with it. Make a snowman. Whatever it is you are doing outside, enjoy and connect to it.

The Illusion of Separation

To quote Guru Pathik again, "The greatest illusion of this world is the illusion of separation." We are not separate from nature and its gifts. Everything, from the tiniest amoeba to the highest mountain, is connected. We are not different from each other, even though we live and behave as if we are. If something affects one thing, it affects us all.

Consider the greenhouse gasses in the ozone layer, along with the immense climate change that is happening right now. Plastic bags have been found in the deepest depths of the ocean due to the rising problem of mass production and waste. Microscopic plastics have now been found in our blood and cannot be filtered out. Extinction rates in the world are skyrocketing. The human race has lost this connection to the earth as a whole due to corporate greed and consumerism. We spend more time inside instead of out, which has messed up our natural sleeping cycles. The world is out of balance, and this is causing devastating effects not just on humanity, but on all the beautiful creatures who live here.

I am not writing these horrible events to scare you, but to make you realize there is no separation between us in the natural world. Spending more time in nature will help you realize this illusion. As you spend more time in nature, you will come to appreciate life in all its forms. By connecting to nature, you can open your third eye chakra.

The earth is calling to you.

Exercise

One of the ways you can spend more time in nature is to exercise in it. As I mentioned before, a good way to implement this technique is to do your yoga outside if you can. Ride your bicycle around the neighborhood. Walk around in your city's local park. Hike in the mountains. Or even do some gardening. If you have children, allow and encourage them to play outside and get dirty, which boosts their natural immunity to viruses and bacteria, according to a Harvard study by Claire McCarthy, a medical doctor. Join them. You will be making memories with them that will last a lifetime. Even if you do not have children, I am sure you have friends or family who do.

No matter what your situation is, there is always a way to go outside and enjoy nature.

Sun and Moon Gazing

Exercising outdoors is an amazing way to be one with nature and open your third eye, but there is another way to enjoy it. You can gaze at the sun and the moon for a couple of minutes. You can watch the sun as it rises, the sun as it sets, or do both on the same day. You will not want to stare directly into the sun and damage your eyes, but a few minutes a day will give you peace of mind. I love watching the sun as it sets over the horizon. When clouds align with the setting sun and the sky lights up like fire, I am astonished over and over again at how beautiful nature is.

Moon gazing is similar. Staring at the moon creates a calming effect on me as well. Gazing at the moon and the stars helps with my perspective of being a piece of the universe experiencing life as a human. As I gaze into the universe, or the little I can see, I realize that I am small and that my issues and struggles are no more than an atom in the expanse of the solar system. This is not to say that they are meaningless, however. Each person's struggle is valid. In the grand scheme of things, they are microscopic.

This realization has helped me gauge my own life and its meaning. Instead of increasing my anxieties, it has shifted my thinking into seeing the bigger picture. This brings peace within me, and my third eye was awakened shortly after I truly felt one with nature.

Write Down Your Dreams

Dream journaling plays a huge part in opening your third eye. Since your pineal gland produces melatonin to produce sleep-inducing chemicals, it also makes sense that it harbors your dreams. According to Sigmund Freud, dreams are the subconscious trying to tell you about the underlying fears, wants, needs, and wishes of your waking life. His book *The Interpretation of Dreams,* published in 1900, analyzes the most common dreams and delves more deeply into their psychoanalysis. It is a reference that is recommended but not required as you explore your dreams and what they mean to you personally.

In one of my counseling sessions, it was recommended that I dream journal as a form of therapy. However, this can also be useful for awakening your third eye. Your third eye is in its natural state when you dream. The more you journal about your dreams, the more connected to your subconscious you become. Keep a notebook and writing utensil by your bed, and upon waking, write down what you remember. This practice can take anywhere from five to fifteen minutes, depending on how much you remember and what your time constraint is.

The more practice you have recalling your dreams, the stronger your connection to your subconscious and the third eye is. If you do not have any notepads or notebooks at home, splurge on a notebook and writing utensil that will trigger you to want to write when you first wake up. I have a notebook on my bedside table that has an image of swirling galaxies on the cover and a pen with a comfortable grip. Nevertheless, whatever you have around your home will surely suffice.

Get Out of Your Comfort Zone

One of the best ways to break free from the repetition of daily life is to try new things and experiences. You learn so much about yourself and the world around you with the introduction of new perspectives. Without new experiences, your life becomes rigid and stale, causing you to feel stuck. Learning more about how other people think, feel, and walk-through life impacts you on a fundamental level. As you open yourself up to these new experiences and perspectives, your third eye senses this new connection to others and emerges from its resting place. Two of the best practices are traveling and discovering new hobbies and activities.

Travel

Traveling is by far the most extreme, and arguably the most useful in opening your third eye. When you travel to different areas of your state/province, country, or even another country or continent altogether, you are expanding your horizons. You learn more about the people who live there and their culture while making friends along the way. This is the epitome of getting out of your comfort zone.

Six years after my divorce, I decided to finally take a trip to Europe, where I had always wanted to visit. Italy was the number one place I wanted to see. The cobblestone streets of Rome greeted me with open arms. Since Rome is a cultural and historical hub in Italy, I frequented many cafes, bars, and restaurants. While there, I learned a portion of the Roman dialect of Italian and conversed with the Romans, American tourists, and even those who were studying abroad at the local universities. It was an amazing and eye-opening experience. My perspectives shifted as I learned more about the history and culture of the city, and that continued while I backpacked across the rest of Europe.

The initial travel overseas is very costly, and I recognize you may not have the financial ability for an extreme measure. There is no shame in having those burdens. As I said before, this can enhance the opening of your third eye and is recommended but not required. Nonetheless, you can have the same type of experiences with traveling in your town or even state/province. Take a new way home while keeping your wits about you. You can also try out a new hangout spot or take a day trip to the next town over with a loved one. Keep an open mind with this step. Make new memories and be open to new experiences. Some people are waiting to meet you.

New Hobbies and Activities

When you travel to another country, you are forced to expand your thinking in order to communicate and connect with other people around you. The same thing goes for trying new things: you are connecting to others. By trying new activities and hobbies, you learn more about who you are and what you like to do. This makes you a more well-rounded person. Have you always wanted to learn to play the ukulele you bought in 2012 but never got around to playing? Enroll in a class or look up videos on YouTube. Gardening? Buy a plant at your local store and cultivate it. Say you're an engineer and you've always wanted to paint. Explore the parts of yourself that are interested in something you've been putting off for a while. Not a good cook? Challenge yourself to make a recipe you always wanted to try, but you were afraid to fail.

You can always pick something at random as well. Maybe it's not something you are particularly interested in or good at. For example, maybe you are a financial whiz who knows more about cryptocurrencies and the current trends in the finance world than most. Your friend is a complete foil to you: maybe they enjoy golfing on the weekends, but you have never done it before. Go with them anyway and experience what they do. You will understand your friend more, and perhaps you will find a new hobby. If you are reading this book and have never attempted to do some of the steps that are mentioned here, that is also an example of getting out of your comfort zone if you decide to follow these steps.

You can either enjoy these new hobbies alone or go with someone you know personally. The important part is to interact with those who are different from you. Learning and growing as a person is an essential part of awakening your third eye. There are many hobbies and activities you can do. A suggestion is to go to your city or town's local coffee shop or recreational center and read some of the events that are happening in your town you do not usually attend. You can either plunge right into it or take it slowly. No matter which way you choose, you are still taking the steps to your awakening.

Eat Healthy Foods

A healthy diet is necessary to sustain your body and remove some of the toxins that are poisoning you. A healthy diet means a longer and more fulfilled life. Food is our lifeblood. The cliche "you are what you eat" is not only a saying but a way of life. If you eat unhealthy food, you are putting in waste and not giving your body what it needs.

Fruits and Vegetables

A vegan or vegetarian diet is not necessary to open your third eye, but the inclusion of healthier foods is. A healthy body is a healthy mind, and vice versa. Personally, I have cut gluten out of my diet because I realized about a year ago, I am allergic. Several of my friends have also gone from being fast food eaters every week to having a vegetarian diet. I will not preach to you about what kind of foods you should be eating. Your body is your own, and you have complete free will to eat the food you want and not feel guilty about it.

If you wish, you can implement some healthier fruits and vegetables that will help with your awakening. Since the colors associated with the sixth chakra are indigo and purple, add some of those to your daily intake of fruits and vegetables. Some purple or blue foods include blueberries, eggplants, purple grapes, and plums.

Purple and blue foods are not the only foods you can supplement your diet with. Other foods that can help awaken your third eye are cilantro, honey, watermelon, lemon, garlic, and dark chocolate. Foods rich in Omega 3s such as avocados and salmon are also a huge plus. A lot of these foods you can use to make smoothies and shakes. Or when you are cooking, add some garlic or lemon to your meal for an extra burst of flavor. Recipes are everywhere online if you are unsure of how to implement some of these foods.

When you are eating these foods, you are decalcifying your pineal gland. Therefore, your third eye blockage will become less as you clear away the physical blockages in your brain. For the freshest produce, either grow your garden if you are able, or shop at a farmer's market.

Foods to Avoid

Foods you will want to avoid are anything that is fast food. You know as well as I do that fast food is not good for you. With the rising epidemic of obesity and the need for convenience, the fast-food industry is still raking in profits of close to $1 trillion (about $3,100 per person in the US) in just 2021 alone. What an insane amount of money! Try to cut down on your spending with fast food as much as you can.

Fast food is not the only culprit here. Most processed foods and extra sugars can hinder your progress as well. Anything containing an absurd amount of high fructose corn syrup or processed sugars can be removed. When looking at the nutrition facts on the side of your food packaging, the ingredients can be found at the bottom. If either high fructose corn syrup or sugar is in the first four mentioned, that means it has the most amount of that ingredient within the food product. Fresh foods are the best foods.

Utilize Crystals

Chances are, if you are looking into the third eye and have conducted some of your own research online, you are very aware of the emphasis on using crystals and essential oils. Essential oils will be covered more in the next section. Keep in mind that these last two sections are not necessary to awaken your third eye, but they can help. You will want to focus more on the lifestyle changes to implement for yourself than relying on crystals. Any crystal that is blue or purple in color will be useful. Amethyst, blue or purple sapphire, sodalite, lapis lazuli, and kyanite are among the most popular.

The crystals and stones mentioned above can be used as a totem. You can either place these directly on top of your third eye or meditate on them. Amethyst is one of the most well-known crystals to open your third eye. Since amethysts are purple, it is said by multiple experts in the metaphysical field that staring at the crystal has helped to unblock their sixth chakra.

Enhance With Essential Oils

Essential oils can also be used in place of crystals. Some essential oils that are useful are lavender, rosemary, sandalwood, and pine. Since your sense of smell is a powerful sensation, it evokes feelings of calmness and enlightenment within you. You can place a couple of drops on your pillow at night, place them on your forehead when you are meditating, or add some when you run a bath at night. With this deep relaxation, your third eye will open more easily. Think of all the different ways you can use this in your own life.

Even if you do not own any essential oils, burning a candle with these same scents can evoke the same feeling. You can burn a lavender candle while you meditate or practice yoga. Bath bombs and Epsom salts infused with lavender or other essential oils help with the deep relaxation your third eye needs to awaken. You can find these at your local supermarket.

Key Takeaways

You now know the top ten steps it takes in order to awaken your third eye. Let us walk through them together.

- The first step is to cement your intent. You will want to know your *why*, as that will keep you going, especially in the beginning when you adjust to your new habits.

- The second task is to start meditating. You can do this by sitting in a quiet place and allowing your mind to empty. You can focus on the color of indigo, your intention for the day, or simply on your breathing. The deep relaxation you feel from meditation will help with the awakening process.

- The third step is sound therapy. While in meditation, you can chant or hum your affirmation out loud. You can also listen to soft music.

- The fourth step is to do some yoga. This stretches out your body and you will be more receptive to the awakening process. The four best poses are the child's pose, head to knee pose, warrior pose, and locust pose.

- The fifth step is to embrace the natural world. Go outside and get some exercise, or simply sit with nature for a few minutes a day. You can also sun and moon gaze.

- The sixth action to take is to write down your dreams. The pineal gland is the most receptive at night. By journaling what you remember of your dreams when you wake up, you are stimulating your third eye.

- The seventh task is to get out of your comfort zone. This can be done by traveling and experiencing other people's and cultures, or by trying out new hobbies and activities. Getting out of your comfort zone forces you to confront your own biases and work through them.

- The eighth step is to eat healthy foods. Eating healthier is better for you as a whole but concentrating on foods good in Omegas 3s and purple or blue in color stimulates your third eye into awakening.

- The ninth task is to utilize crystals. Crystals such as amethyst and sapphires are among the most common and can be used during meditation.

- The tenth and final step is to enhance with essential oils such as lavender and sandalwood. You can place a few drops on your pillow or in your bath. Candles, bath bombs, and Epsom salts are useful for deep relaxation.

Now that you know the steps to awaken your third eye, take a few moments to reflect on how you can implement these strategies into your own life. Life is messy and crazy, but with some time set aside, you will be able to open your third eye when you are ready. Are you ready to know what to expect once it is opened? Continue reading to find out.

Chapter 3:

What to Expect

Erica Matluck, a licensed naturopathic doctor and nurse practitioner, says, "an open third eye sees the world for the stage it is." With an opened third eye, you will be able to see the truths of the world and the universe you could not before. The awakening process can be terrifying at first, but the result is so worth it. You want the experience to feel more and see more than you ever thought possible. You know yourself more. Once the sixth chakra is unblocked, you will receive a new spiritual authenticity.

This last chapter includes what to fully expect from an opened third eye: the benefits as well as the possible negative outcomes. To prepare for this experience, you should learn all you can before doing so. Preparation is the key to success. Opening your third eye is no different.

Maslow's Hierarchy of Needs

Self-actualization is the last tier in Maslow's hierarchy of needs. It is a pyramid that builds off of each foundation. It has been theorized that once one tier is met, the next is to pursue the next level.

This is very similar to the seven chakras and what they are associated with. You will notice some of the basic needs of each tier in the pyramid are fundamental to proceeding with self-actualization. While there are seven chakras, the hierarchy only has five tiers to live a fulfilled life.

There are five levels, each with a specific need that must be met. The bottom of the pyramid is your survival needs: food, water, shelter, and sleep. To exist as a human being, these needs must be met. The next is safety and security. This manifests within the home itself: shelter from the elements, protection from violence and sickness, or even financial and job security. You must be able to feel safe and protected to pursue the next tier, which is love. To be able to give and receive love, you must first feel safe and secure. This love stems from friends, family, and intimate partners. In this tier, you feel a sense of belonging to a group or a community. The fourth tier is your esteem needs: the need to give respect to yourself as well as others. You also need to receive respect, which can manifest as recognition from others and confidence from yourself.

Self-actualization is the last tier, and the one most closely related to opening the third eye chakra. Self-actualization occurs when you figure out who you are and what you want from life. This is where you are the best version of yourself: your full potential. You pursue your dreams, find your passions, and seek the happiness you have been chasing your entire life. Once the third eye is opened, this need is also met, and you have achieved higher consciousness.

Opened Third Eye

Now that the blockages are cleared, the energy flows down the metaphorical creek. When the third eye is opened, you will come to find your intuition, wisdom, and guidance have drastically increased. You are more in balance with your thoughts and emotions. For the first time in your life, you will have a clear sense of what your passions are and the meaning of your life's work. This is you, unapologetically. You are not your judgments, your fears, your beliefs, or thoughts. Your previous self-identity fractures once the chakra starts to open, and it shatters completely once it is fully unblocked.

Nothing will be the same. Thinking about the truths of yourself and the universe can be terrifying. Your inner being is calling out to you, begging you to let go of everything you thought you knew. Your feelings of fear are valid; there is nothing scarier than letting go of who you thought you are to reveal who you are. Not only that, but you will see people for who they are. You will not be easily fooled or lied to, and this can cause friction between you and your loved ones. You must surrender yourself and let go.

Benefits of Awakening Your Third Eye

The benefits far outweigh the negative aspects of awakening the third eye chakra. Once it is opened, you are more in tune with yourself and the world around you. The mirror you once saw yourself in was a reflection of the person you thought you were. Now that it is shattered, lying on the floor, you can let go of this attachment to yourself. There is nothing more freeing than witnessing the bleeding and broken version of you from before and transforming into another version of you. You are stronger, braver, fearless, with a deep motivation you have never been able to conjure before. You are still you, but *better*. You are one with the universe. You are whole.

Achieved Higher Consciousness

I have mentioned higher consciousness several times within this book, but the burning question remains: what is it? Higher consciousness may seem like a mystical and magical power, but that is not the case. It simply means being fully present at the moment and allowing your ego to sit on the sidelines. Instead of focusing on "I/me," you are more in tune with your surroundings and yourself. It is the inner peace you crave, to sit comfortably with yourself in silence.

Many people are afraid to be alone with their thoughts. You are in constant movement with them, buzzing and burning in your mind like wasps swarming and stinging you. Your anxiety over your next movement causes unrest. The ego within you wants to maintain control, focusing on the narrow-minded version of yourself. It wants you to concentrate on it instead of what you do and how it affects others in the world. You are not in control; your ego is not in control. You are a spiritual entity experiencing life as a human, not the other way around.

When you have achieved higher consciousness, the wasps buzzing in your brain slow down to a lazy bumblebee gathering pollen from flower to flower. You have a clearer, serene mind. Your thoughts are no longer a necessity, but instead tools to use when you need them. Fully understanding your thoughts and feelings will help you make better decisions.

Intuition Improvement

When your third eye is opened, your intuition improves. Intuition is when you can quickly process information and make judgments on that information, synonymous with trusting your gut. Intuition can be an inexplicable feeling of impending doom when a situation feels off. I am sure you can relate to this within your own life and experiences. There is what feels like a pit in your stomach, and you cannot shake it off. Your head and heart are at war because something does not add up. This is your intuition.

Intuition can also lead you down the road you were meant to be on. With this trust and faith in yourself, you are now able to forge a new path of truth and enlightenment. You should be confident with yourself to know what your life's purpose is and what your personal, professional, and financial goals are.

Once you open your third eye, you can trust yourself and see those around you who are not good for you. By now, you understand the motivations of yourself and those around you, and your decisions will be made from forethought and logic instead of driven by fear. You gain the ability to trust your gut with newly founded intuition.

Positive Outlook

In addition to the improvement of your intuition, you will also gain a more positive outlook on life. Because you now have the inner peace you so desperately craved, your outlook is more positive. Suddenly, the clouds have disappeared in your mind and your heart, allowing the sun to shine on perceived bleak experiences. You are happy. Imagine what this happiness and contentment with life means to you. The world could use a little more positivity and light within it. Use that light within you to immerse yourself in the world. Your boundaries are set; your sense of self-worth and respect flow through you.

When you have a positive outlook on life, your ability to manage the stresses in your life increases. This reduces the health effects of the stresses that come from living in this world such as cardiovascular diseases, strokes, and respiratory infections. When your third eye is opened from a negative mindset, such as limiting beliefs and self-talk, as well as incomplete or misconstrued information, you are more able to shift this negativity into well-balanced intuition.

Lucid Dreaming

While this can be considered a superpower, so to speak, lucid dreaming is also a benefit from opening your third eye. Lucid dreaming is when you are in control of your dreams in the literal sense. This feeds into your awareness and self-control in the waking world. The third eye is the epitome of the dream world. Since the third eye is in direct contact with the pineal gland, it gives the ability to produce more lucid dreams.

When you lucid dream and are in control of your actions within the dream, you can overcome phobias and nightmares. Since you make your own rules within the dream space, you are enhancing your creativity. When this happens, you can thank yourself for the commitment to awakening your third eye.

Psychic Abilities

Along with these benefits, the most well-known benefit is the newfound psychic abilities. These abilities tend to be more open to those who can see through time and space. Some are born with this gift; others take years to cultivate. Do not be alarmed if gifts such as clairvoyance are not present immediately, if they ever are materialized. Psychic abilities are an advanced stage. This should not bum you out, but instead, appreciate the fact your third eye is open and receptive to the universe around you. If and when you happen to come across these gifts either within yourself or another, remember it is the highest elevation of the third eye you can experience.

Possible Negative Experiences

Just as with any new experience, it is best to be prepared for the problems that can arise from them. Opening your third eye is an intense undertaking not for the faint of heart. You must be fully ready to receive the gifts that are given to you. As mentioned before, it is highly recommended that you open the other five chakras before opening this one. There are disturbing consequences for those who do not.

The same is true for forcing your third eye to open. Oftentimes, when you force the eye open before it is ready, it can have devastating lasting effects on the person and their consciousness. The issue here is when you are not ready, and you keep forcing it open to satisfy your ego. The opening backfires on you. Your dreams darken into nightmares, and it is possible to lose touch with reality.

Those who do not heed these warnings suffer greatly. I do not say this lightly. There are instances where people have reported some of these experiences and what they can do to your mind.

Headaches

Headaches are among the most common side effects of awakening your third eye before it is ready to open. The energy that is stuck in your third eye is less like a calm swirling creek and more like a whirlpool. The energy within has no place to go, and this can cause headaches and migraines of varying intensity and frequency. Keep in mind that this can also happen when your third eye is opened when it is ready due to the influx of information. There will be more in-depth analysis in the section on sensory overload.

Nightmares and Sleeping Difficulties

Nightmares are also relatively common. When you open your eye before it is ready to see, there are dire consequences. We share the universe with other, more terrifying beings such as demons and fourth-dimensional beings. What you think is lucid dreaming can swiftly shift to nightmares in the metaphorical blink of an eye. Now that you can see the other beings who rule the universe with us, there is no doubt this is a terrifying experience. Since the third eye has been awakened, you are more susceptible to receiving messages from these interdimensional beings.

Along with your nightmares, you will face difficulties falling and staying asleep. This walks hand-in-hand with your nightmares. There can be several reasons for this, also tying into the next section of too much stimulation to your senses in the waking world. Sometimes, you may be accompanied by unwanted, terrifying creatures. Sleep paralysis can also be defined as difficulties falling and staying asleep because of the aforementioned demons.

Sensory Overload

When your third eye is opened, your senses can be overwhelmed. At first, the changes are small; you can smell things you could not before or even hear things whispered in your ear. The colors and lights of the world blind you, which can cause the headaches previously discussed. You may be able to feel something touching you that is not there, which I call phantom touching. There have even been reports of increased paranoia because you know you are being watched, but no one else can see. While being able to see auras and chakras can be considered a bonus when your third eye opens, beings from other planes of existence are with you as well. A demon or fourth-dimensional being may be observing you, which is frightening to even think about.

Fear and Anxieties

So far, all of these negative effects on you all tie into one major side effect: fear and anxieties. When your senses are overloaded, it causes extreme amounts of stress and paranoia. When the third eye is awakened before its time, delusions start to creep in, and soon you will be unable to decipher fact from fiction in extreme cases. This is also true for difficulties falling and staying asleep paired with nightmares. Basically, if you open your third eye before it is time to, you will face an unprecedented amount of fear and anxiety.

When this happens, your natural instinct is to isolate yourself from family and loved ones who have not gone through these same experiences. They will have difficulty relating to you and even being there for you when you need them. Extreme fear and anxiety can prevent you from leading a normal life. They may see this as canceling plans for no reason, even though you are experiencing a magnitude of personality shifts. These bizarre and chaotic shifts in your behavior may cause them to essentially give up on you, therefore ending relationships because they cannot handle your inconsistencies. If you are suffering from depression, consider this synonymous with an extreme depressive episode.

Remember, however, to keep in mind that, although anxieties and fears are commonplace, the intensity of these fears and anxieties is not. They are the outliers of this side effect. Despite this, it is important to be aware because you do not know how you will react to these experiences.

Astral Projection

Astral projection is when you have an out-of-body experience. This usually happens when you are asleep.

When you awaken, your soul is separated from your body, and therefore, you can see yourself sleeping. In theory, this sounds pretty cool. Not only see yourself sleeping, but you can come back with the wisdom and knowledge of the universe. In practice is where things can be frightening, especially if it is sudden and unwanted. When the soul leaves the body, it transcends into other planes of existence. These astral planes can be located on earth or anywhere in the universe. The spirit is more susceptible to energy attacks as it travels through astral planes.

The biggest danger with this is your physical body remains vulnerable in the physical world. This is similar to Aang's Spirit World adventures in the show *Avatar: The Last Airbender*. When he goes into the Spirit World to find answers to some of the real-world problems, it is only his spirit that leaves. His physical body remains in meditation. The show emphasizes this. If the body is harmed or moved, his soul cannot return to his body if he cannot find it. Typically, this does not happen; your physical body remains in bed but is vulnerable to harm.

Spiritual Awakening

At this point, you should have six of the seven chakras opened and ready to receive spiritual awakening. With the opening of your third eye, you should have been given access to the various benefits, including spiritual awakening. Spiritual awakening is when you have epiphanies and breakthroughs into what spirituality means to you personally. You are now consciously aware of ideas and perspectives that we did not realize there were. In essence, this is our one true self. We are no longer bound to the self the ego has control over. You are much more self-aware and can let go of attachments that have held you in a state of stagnation.

Because you have undergone such a massive transformation, your true self shines forth. At this point, you have let go of your past unhealthy habits and attachments. You now can connect and empathize with others from all walks of life. Compassion and empathy for others allow you to be more in tune with the world around you. With this true self and unlocked intuition, you can see the authenticity in others. The relationships you may have lost during your transformation can now be replaced with those who are truly genuine.

Closing Your Third Eye

Now that you have opened your third eye and have experienced a spiritual awakening, it may be difficult to close. If the third eye is opened before it is ready, and therefore you are experiencing negative side effects, it may be wise to close it again. This can be caused by overuse and misuse, further draining you. It is a personal choice. For example, you may no longer wish to receive messages from other beings. Remember that closing the third eye completely is not recommended. Think of your third eye as a muscle that has not been used for a long time and you start working it out again. If you overuse it, your pains will be far greater than building it up gradually. Experimenting with your third eye in excess in a relatively short amount of time can cause some of the previous side effects as well.

If you decide to close your third eye, talk to your spiritual guide first before attempting to close it on your own. You may need extra guidance for leveling the intense experiences you are facing. One way you can close it is to visualize your third eye being covered or closed. You can also do this by closing your eyes and conducting this same visualization, but also placing your palm against your forehead.

Key Takeaways

Since you have used the tools and steps to awaken your third eye, it is crucial to know what to expect after it is opened. The key things you need to know are as follows:

- In order to achieve self-actualization, your other needs must be met according to Maslow's hierarchy of needs. Self-actualization is the last step.

- When the third eye is awakened, you will feel different. You may feel lighter and freer after all the negativity from your previous life has been washed away.

- Some of the benefits of third eye awakening are higher consciousness, increased intuition, a positive outlook, lucid dreaming, and depending on the advancement of your opened third eye, psychic abilities.

- Possible negative side effects include headaches, nightmares, and sleeping problems, sensory overload, fear and anxieties, and astral projection. These side effects are usually the result of not opening the previous chakras or attempting to open the third eye before it is ready.

- Once you have mastered opening your third eye, it may be difficult to close. You are now your true self, which will either help you or hinder you. It may be wise to close it for a while to not receive any more negative side effects.

Now that you are towards the end of your initial spiritual journey, the next step is to maintain the awakening you have. Continue with the practices and steps that work best for you.

Conclusion

Self-help author Mwanandeke Kindembo of Congo writes, "The so-called 'third eye' is not an eye in itself, but a gateway to infinity or self-realization." This quote is a wonderful summation of everything you have learned in this book. It reflects that the third eye is not an actual eye but is the center of the soul to receive higher consciousness, a new perspective, and a newfound spiritual awakening. In order to do this, there are things to remember before, during, and after your eventual spiritual awakening.

Before Awakening

In order to awaken your third eye, you must remember to open the previous five chakras: the root, sacral, solar plexus, heart, and throat chakras. Each chakra is opened and blocked in its own special ways. You must first ground yourself in these chakras, taking care to open each slowly and when it is time. A spiritual guide with experience in helping others find their way through a third eye opening can be beneficial to your unique journey. Potential dangers include nightmares and delusions.

The pineal gland and the third eye are connected. Since the third eye is located directly in the center of your forehead, the spiritual energy within your third eye swirls around in your pineal gland. It is the part of your brain that produces melatonin, the chemical in your brain that signals you when to fall asleep. In order to nurture this part of your brain, place your phone in another room an hour before going to bed. Foods such as those rich in Omega 3s along with fresh fruits and vegetables can help with the decalcification in your pineal gland. This in turn can make the process of opening your third eye easier.

Since you have picked up this book, your third eye is closed. Symptoms can manifest in both your physical body and your mental health. Physically, you can feel drained with head and backaches since the third eye is associated with the nervous system. Mentally, these symptoms can manifest similar to depression and other mood disorders. Keep in mind that attempting to open your third eye is no substitute for mental healthcare professionals. The blockage within your third eye can also be caused by hardships and not being true to who you are.

10 Steps to Awakening

In order to open your third eye, I recommend ten easy-to-implement steps. The first is to cement your intent. Figuring out why it is you want to open your third eye will be the foundation when you are feeling discouraged with the process. The next step is to say out loud your affirmations. Pair this with the next step of meditation.

You can meditate on the color indigo, on your affirmations, on your intent, or even in silence. It is your own personal preference. Sound therapy such as chanting or humming while meditating stimulates your pineal gland, which allows your third eye to open more easily.

Yoga is the fourth step to unlocking your third eye's potential. There are four yoga poses that can help with this process: the child's pose, head to knee pose, warrior pose, and locust pose.

The fifth step is to embrace the natural world through exercise, or just simply sitting outside in nature. The key here is to reflect on the earth and its wonders. You can also try sun and moon gazing. You can implement these four steps into a minimum of 30 minutes a day combined by budgeting out a time that works best for you. As long as you make the commitment and effort, you should be able to find some time.

The sixth step is to write down your dreams. Whenever you wake up, take about ten minutes to jot down what you can remember from your dreams. This helps to awaken your third eye since your dream state is where its home is.

The seventh step is to get out of your comfort zone. This can be done by traveling cross-country, to another country, or even across your state or province. Find new activities and hobbies that you enjoy. The important part here is to expand our horizons to gain a different perspective on others' lives.

The eighth step is to eat healthier foods. You might want to concentrate on the colors blue and purple and implement those in your diet. Other foods such as salmon rich in Omega 3s can help with this process as well.

The ninth and tenth steps to opening your third eye are utilizing crystals and enhancing with essential oils. These steps are an additive and not required but can help with third eye awakening. Using crystals and essential oils while you meditate is a great way to complement each other. You can also use essential oils in a relaxing bath.

After Awakening

After opening your third eye, you may find that you have shed the old you and become your true self. You have now achieved self-actualization now that all your needs have been met, according to Maslow's hierarchy of needs. You may feel lighter and freer than you have ever felt before. Some of the benefits of opening your third eye are higher consciousness, increased intuition, a positive outlook, lucid dreaming, and even psychic abilities.

There is a caution to be had if you awaken your third eye before it is time to. Some of these negative side effects are headaches, nightmares and sleeping problems, sensory overload, fear and anxieties, and astral projection. If you feel you must, you are able to close your third eye if you are experiencing some of these negative side effects, especially those that are more severe.

Once you have mastered your spiritual awakening, you are now able to reflect on how the experience changed you.

Reflect on Your Journey

This is it. You've transformed from your ego self to your true self. Your genuine love for life shines through, giving you the power to let go of the things you thought mattered but, in reality, did not. For the first time in your life, you feel whole and certain of yourself.

How does it make you feel?

Take some time to journal on the journey from the person you were to the person you are now. How much have you grown? Changed? Do you regret it? Was it a sudden, drastic change, or did you take it slow?

It is important to reflect on how the experience shattered you. What worked for you? What advice would you give to others who want to go on a similar journey?

If you were ready for your spiritual awakening, you were at your lowest point. When we are at our lowest point, there is a higher chance to be more open to change. What encouraged you to make this change for yourself?

Whether you experienced psychic powers or interdimensional beings, do not be afraid to tell others what you went through. Your third eye is now open; you should have no qualms with revealing the truth as you experienced it.

So, the question now is: What will you do with it?

References

Brunton, S. (n.d.). *Third Eye Opening Symptoms And Its Dangers*. Retrieved April 1, 2022, from https://www.spiritualunite.com/articles/third-eye-awakening-symptoms-and-its-dangers/

Cameron, Y. (2022, February 2). *Third-Eye Chakra Healing for Beginners*. Mindbodygreen. https://www.mindbodygreen.com/0-97/Third-Eye-Chakra-Healing-for-Beginners.html

DiMartino, M. D., & Konietzko, B. (2006, December 1). "The Guru". *Avatar: The Last Airbender*. [Fantasy]. https://www.youtube.com/watch?v=cH-HT9WCtiQ

Hurst, C. (2017, October 19). *Chakra Healing For Beginners: How To Open Your Third Eye*. The Law Of Attraction. https://www.thelawofattraction.com/third-eye-chakra-healing/

Jain, R. (2020, October 7). *Ajna: How To Feel & Heal The Third Eye Chakra*. https://www.mindbodygreen.com/0-97/Third-Eye-Chakra-Healing-for-Beginners.html

Kabic, J. (2021, August 15). Spiritual Awakening [Symptoms, Stages & How to Experience It]. *Review42*. https://review42.com/resources/spiritual-awakening/

Lucid Dream Society. (n.d.). *Lucid Dreaming Benefits: 13 Odd But Amazing Uses - Lucid Dream Society*. Retrieved April 8, 2022, from https://luciddreamsociety.com/lucid-dreaming-benefits/

Luna, A. (2022, March 25). *The Ultimate Guide to Third Eye Chakra Healing For Complete Beginners*. LonerWolf. https://lonerwolf.com/third-eye-chakra-healing/

Maize, K. (n.d.). *Meditate and Unblock Your Chakras: Avatar the Last Airbender Style*. Retrieved April 1, 2022, from https://www.kelleemaize.com/post/meditate-and-unblock-your-chakras-avatar-the-last-airbender-style

Matluck, E. (2019, July 25). *Third Eye Chakra: A Deep Dive Into What It Is + How To Unblock It | mindbodygreen*. https://www.mindbodygreen.com/articles/third-eye-chakra-4-techniques-for-opening-up-the-sixth-chakra

Mayo Clinic Staff. (n.d.). *How to stop negative self-talk*. Mayo Clinic. Retrieved April 8, 2022, from https://www.mayoclinic.org/healthy-lifestyle/stress-management/in-depth/positive-thinking/art-20043950

McCarthy, C., MD. (2018, May 22). *6 reasons children need to play outside*. Harvard Health. https://www.health.harvard.edu/blog/6-reasons-children-need-to-play-outside-2018052213880

McCay, F. (2022, March 29). *47+ Fast Food Industry Statistics 2021 [Order Up!]*. SpendMeNot. https://spendmenot.com/blog/fast-food-industry-statistics/

Mellor, S. (2022, March 26). *Tiny particles of plastic just got found inside humans for the first time*. Fortune. https://fortune.com/2022/03/24/tiny-microplastics-particles-human-blood/

Murphy, A. (2020, October 26). *How to Awaken Your Third Eye aka the Pineal Gland | Gaia*. https://www.gaia.com/article/how-to-awaken-your-third-eye

O, J. (2020, December 15). 10 Ways To Open Your Third Eye Chakra. *L'Aquila Active*. https://laquilaactive.com/10-ways-to-open-your-third-eye-chakra/

Oddo, E. (n.d.). *Spiritual Awakening: 3 books in 1: Your complete guide to healing yourself through Chakras for Beginners, Third Eye for Beginners and Reiki for Beginners.*
https://books.google.com/books?hl=en&lr=&id=JDBdEAAAQBAJ&oi=fnd&pg=PT3&dq=third+eye+awakening&ots=Ra5XOVGEpU&sig=OavbBX6_pcJhjad4ez_hqF_wyUY#v=onepage&q=third%20eye%20awakening&f=false

Sagan, S. (2007). *Awakening The Third Eye*. 279.

Schneider, A., & Cooper, N. J. (2019). *A Brief History of the Chakras in Human Body* (Article 16, Vol. 15). pp. 21-27. https://doi.org/10.13140/RG.2.2.17372.00646

Seventh Wonder. (2018, June 9). *Understanding Your Third Eye Chakra | Seventh Wonder Holistic Spa*. https://seventh-wonder.com/understanding-your-third-eye-chakra/

Shahjee, A. (n.d.). Third Eye Awakening. *Shahjee*. Retrieved April 1, 2022, from http://www.shahjee.org/third-eye-awakening/

Shoja, M. M., Hoepfer, L. D., & Agutter, P. S. (2015, March 11). *History of the pineal gland | SpringerLink*. https://link.springer.com/article/10.1007/s00381-015-2636-3

Singh, J. (2020, January 25). Awakening the Third Eye (Ajna) Chakra (The Eye of Shiva). *MindfulnessQuest*. https://mindfulnessquest.com/awakening-the-third-eye-chakra/

Stokes, V. (2021, May 6). *How to Open Your Third Eye Chakra for Spiritual Awakening*. https://www.healthline.com/health/mind-body/how-to-open-your-third-eye#takeaway

Team SEEMA. (2021, September 23). The Beginner's Guide to the Third Eye Chakra. *Seema*. https://www.seema.com/the-beginners-guide-to-the-third-eye-chakra/

Printed in Great Britain
by Amazon